Hooray for Orchards!

A Bobbie Kalman Book

Crabtree Publishing Company

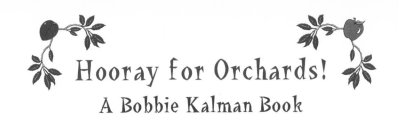

Hooray for Orchards!
A Bobbie Kalman Book

In memory of Jim Larin

Editor-in-Chief
Bobbie Kalman

Writing team
Bobbie Kalman
Allison Larin
Niki Walker

Managing editor
Lynda Hale

Text and photo research
Allison Larin

Editors
Niki Walker
Greg Nickles

Computer design
Lynda Hale
Campbell Creative Services

Production coordinator
Hannelore Sotzek

Printer
Worzalla Publishing Company

Color separations and film
Dot 'n Line Image Inc.
CCS Princeton (cover)

Special thanks to
Megan Peters and Danielle Kessel (the models who appear on the cover);
Karen McMillan; Hilary Whitty and Petra Mindorff; B. Milewicz of
Milewicz Orchards; Ken Slingerland, Gerry Walker, Tom Ferencevic,
Mike Dumoulin, and Bernie Solymar of OMAFRA; Sandra Hawkins of
Ontario Agri-Food Education; Jordan Frozen Foods Limited; David
Dionne and Dionne Farm; Kurtz Farm; Joyette Haron; Whitty Farms;
Jim Rainforth and Gail Anderson of the Ontario Tender Fruit
Producers' Marketing Board

Photographs
AGstockUSA: David Frazier: page 16; Ed Young: page 8 (bottom)
Marc Crabtree: pages 30, 31
Giraudon/Art Resource, NY: page 5
Bobbie Kalman: front and back covers
Diane Payton Majumdar: title page, pages 8 (top), 14, 20,
    22, 25, 26, 27 (all), 28
Tom McHugh/Photo Researchers, Inc.: page 17
Ken Slingerland/Ontario Ministry of Agriculture, Food
    and Rural Affairs: pages 11, 18, 19, 21, 23, 24

Illustrations
All illustrations by Barbara Bedell except the following:
    Cori Marvin: page 9

Consultants
Teacher Consultants from Ontario Agri-Food Education

Crabtree Publishing Company

350 Fifth Avenue
Suite 3308
New York
N.Y. 10118

360 York Road, RR 4,
Niagara-on-the-Lake,
Ontario, Canada
L0S 1J0

73 Lime Walk
Headington
Oxford OX3 7AD
United Kingdom

Cataloging in Publication Data
Kalman, Bobbie
    Hooray for orchards!

(Hooray for farming!)
Includes index.

ISBN 0-86505-653-6 (library bound)   ISBN 0-86505-667-6 (pbk.)
This book introduces aspects of orchards, including pollination,
trees, fruit development, grafting, fruit processing, pests, pesticides,
and harvesting. Includes simple recipes using fruit.

1. Fruit-culture—Juvenile literature. 2. Orchards—Juvenile literature.
3. Fruit—Juvenile literature. [1. Fruit culture. 2. Orchards. 3. Fruit.]
I. Title. II. Series: Kalman, Bobbie. Hooray for farming!

SB357.2.K35   1997   j634   LC 97-31451
                                                            CIP

Orchards in bloom

What are orchards?

All the fruit that people buy at a market or grocery store comes from farms. The farmers who run fruit farms are called **fruit growers**. A place where fruit is grown on trees is called an **orchard**. A fruit grower can grow apples, pears, peaches, plums, or cherries in an orchard.

Orchards today

Long ago, families grew their own fruit. Today, some families still have a few fruit trees growing in their yard, but most people do not grow their own fruit. They buy the fruit that is grown in orchards.

Hooray for fruit growers!

Every time you bite into an apple or other fruit, be thankful that someone grew it for you. Think of all the things you use every day that are made from fruit. Juice, pies, cakes, and jam are just a few of these. The next time you eat a cherry or peach pie, shout "Hooray for orchards! Hooray for fruit growers!"

In the past, a family picked fruit from their fruit trees in the summer. They ate some of the fruit and made the rest into jam and preserves that could be used throughout the winter.

Kinds of fruit

Fruit is divided into groups. Pomes, stone fruits, berries, aggregates, and citrus are examples of different fruit groups. Some fruits, such as pineapples, belong to their own group.

Pomes

Pomes have **cores** with several small seeds inside. The **flesh** is crunchy, and the skin is thin. Apples and pears are both pomes.

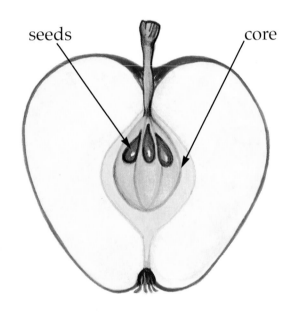

seeds   core

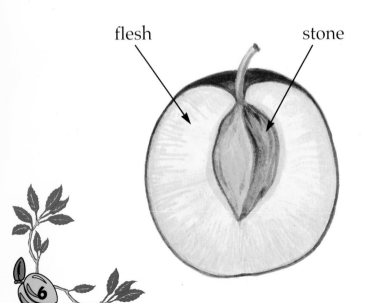

flesh   stone

Stone fruits

Stone fruits have soft flesh, a thin skin, and a **stone** in the center. Peaches, plums, and cherries are stone fruits.

Berries

Berries have soft, juicy flesh and very thin skin. Most have tiny seeds in their center. The seeds are so small that most people do not notice them at all. Grapes, blueberries, and currants are examples of berries.

Aggregates

Some aggregates have seeds on the outside of their skin. Strawberries and raspberries are types of aggregates.

Citrus

Citrus fruits have many separate sections inside a tough outer skin. Citrus fruits grow only in very warm places such as Florida and California. Oranges, lemons, limes, and grapefruits are all citrus fruits.

Where does fruit grow?

Different kinds of fruits grow on different kinds of plants. Some berries, such as grapes, grow on **vines**. Some, such as blueberries, grow on bushes. Aggregates also grow on bushes or small plants.

*Strawberries grow on small plants in berry **fields** like this one. Raspberries grow on larger bushes.*

Citrus fruits grow on trees. The trees grow in special orchards called **groves**. This book is about how pomes and stone fruits grow. They are the fruits we find in orchards.

Fruit varieties

There are **varieties** of each fruit. Varieties are types of one fruit. For example, there are varieties of apples. **Spartan** apples are red, **Granny Smith** apples are green, and **Golden Delicious** apples are yellow.

Which variety?

The varieties that a fruit grower decides to grow depend on many things. A grower must make sure to choose a variety that grows well in the area where he or she lives. Most growers choose a variety they know people want to buy. Some varieties are more popular than others, and some sell for more money.

What do orchards need?

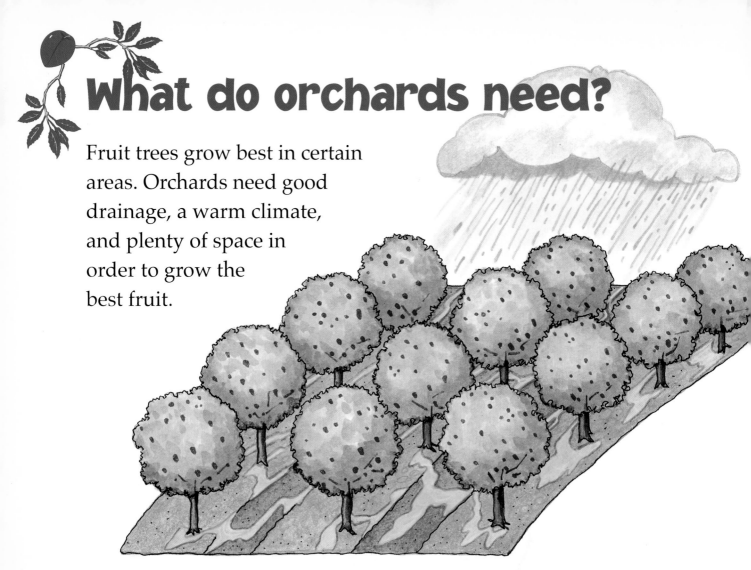

Fruit trees grow best in certain areas. Orchards need good drainage, a warm climate, and plenty of space in order to grow the best fruit.

Drainage

Orchards need good **drainage**. Land on a gentle slope is an ideal place to plant an orchard. Water runs down the slope slowly. The trees soak up enough water to stay healthy and grow, but the ground around the trees does not get soggy. Fruit trees do not grow well in wet ground.

Climate

Orchards also need a specific **climate**. A climate is the usual weather in a particular area. California and Florida have warm weather, so they have a warm climate. Most orchards need a moderate climate, which is neither too hot in the summer nor too cold in the winter. They also need plenty of sunlight.

Roomy rows

The trees in orchards need space between them so that their roots have room to spread. The fruit grower must be able to drive a tractor or truck between the trees without hitting them. Hitting the trees could break their branches or damage the fruit growing on them.

How fruit trees grow

Most farmers do not grow their fruit trees from seeds. It takes many years for the seed from a fruit to grow into a tree. When a seed is planted, it breaks open, and roots grow down into the soil. A stem, or trunk, slowly grows up through the ground.

12

Grafting

Most farmers buy young fruit trees that have been **grafted**. A grafted tree is made up of two trees that have been cut to fit together. Grafted trees are stronger and healthier and grow better fruit than trees that are not grafted.

How grafting is done

When trees are grafted, the bottom part of one tree is already planted in soil when it is cut. The other tree's trunk and branches are then joined with the bottom tree. The joint is covered with wax and then wrapped with a bandage. The two pieces slowly grow into one tree.

Flowering to fruit

Each spring, the trees in an orchard grow small flowers called **blossoms**. Blossoms turn into fruit. The fruit carries the seeds that will grow into new trees.

Pollination

Blossoms become fruit only if they are **pollinated**. Pollination happens when the **pollen** from one blossom reaches the **stigma** of another blossom. Pollen is a yellow powder found on the **stamens** of a blossom. Once a blossom is pollinated, its petals fall off. The blossom's ovaries grow larger and become a fruit.

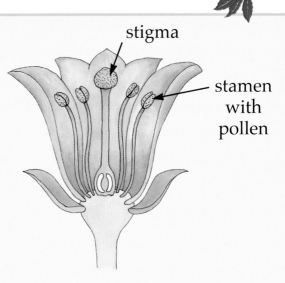

stigma

stamen with pollen

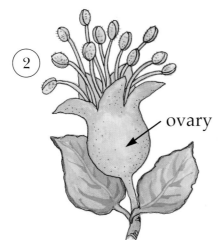

ovary

1. These apple blossoms have been pollinated.
2. The petals have fallen off this blossom. The ovary grows bigger.
3. The ovary grows even larger as seeds grow inside it.
4. The ovary finally becomes an apple, and the ovules have become the seeds.

The pollinators

Pollen has to be moved from one blossom to another. Bees do this job. Bees need the nectar found in blossoms to make honey, and they visit all the blossoms they can. As they collect nectar, they get covered with pollen. When the bees fly from blossom to blossom, pollen rubs off their body and pollinates the blossoms. Many fruit growers pay beekeepers to bring honeybees to their orchard. They want to make sure that there are a lot of bees in their orchard to pollinate the blossoms. The more blossoms that are pollinated, the more fruit the grower will have to sell.

Caring for orchards

To keep their orchards in good shape, fruit growers have many jobs to do throughout the year. They want to make sure that the fruit growing in their orchards will be big and healthy. They want the fruit to look good. Big, tasty fruit sells at a higher price than small fruit.

Thinning trees
When a tree has too much fruit growing on it, its branches sometimes break. The farmer has to **thin** the tree to keep the branches from snapping. Thinning is taking the extra fruit off branches. It gives the fruit left on the tree more room to grow.

Watering the orchard

Most orchards do not get enough water
from rain. Fruit growers bring extra water
to their orchards using pipes and machines.
Powerful sprinklers spray the water over
all the trees.

Mowing

Long grass and weeds grow between trees. The fruit grower must make sure the orchard is mowed often during the spring and summer. Mowing the grass and weeds keep them from taking important nutrients out of the ground. Fruit trees need a lot of nutrients in order to grow healthy, tasty fruit.

Pruning

Each spring, the fruit grower **prunes** the fruit trees, or cuts off many of their branches. In the past, trees were allowed to grow so big that people had to use tall ladders to reach all the fruit growing on them. Pruning keeps trees small. Smaller trees are easy to reach from the ground or a short ladder. Pruning also gets rid of dead and broken branches. After these branches are cut off, all of the tree's energy goes to the healthy, fruit-producing branches. The energy is not wasted on branches that are no longer growing fruit.

Pests and diseases

Insects, birds, and other pests damage the fruit growing in an orchard. Diseases can also ruin the fruit. Damaged fruit cannot be sold. Some diseases destroy fruit completely. Others kill the trees. Protecting trees from these problems is an important part of a fruit grower's job.

Keeping pests away

Mice, rabbits, and deer eat the bark off tree trunks. A tree dies if it loses too much bark. Farmers can wrap plastic or metal around the bottom of tree trunks to stop pests from reaching the bark. Some growers paint the bottom of their tree trunks. Painted bark does not make a tasty snack! Birds love to eat cherries and plums. To keep birds away, some farmers place loud noise-makers or scarecrows in their orchards.

Spraying

To prevent diseases and kill insect pests, most fruit growers spray their fruit with chemicals. These chemicals are called **pesticides.** Pesticides are sprayed on fruit trees several times during the spring and summer.

Harvesting the fruit

From July to October, the fruit growing in orchards is **harvested**, or picked from the trees. Not all the fruit on a tree is ripe enough to be picked at the same time. Each tree is harvested at least three times so that no fruit is picked too soon or too late.

Harvested by hand

Most fruit is harvested by hand. People stand on short ladders or platforms to reach it. They pull or twist the fruit off the branch and put it into baskets or boxes. Some fruits must be handled gently so that they do not bruise.

Using machines

Tart or sour cherries are harvested by a machine. The machine shakes the tree trunk so that the cherries fall off the branches. The cherries drop onto a slanted platform and roll into bins of water below. Tart cherries are not bruised by falling, rolling, and landing in water.

Migrant workers

Many fruit growers need extra help caring for their orchards. They often hire **migrant workers**. Migrant workers are people who move from place to place to work on farms. They follow the growing seasons in different areas of the country.

Migrant workers prune the trees, thin them, spray them, and harvest the fruit. They are hired for only part of the year, until the harvest is finished. They then move to an area where other farmers need help. Migrant workers help grow much of the fruit you eat. Shout "Hooray for migrant workers!"

Where does the fruit go?

After being picked, most fruit is washed before it leaves the farm. People sort through the fruit and take out any that are rotten or damaged. Some of the fruit is put into boxes, loaded onto a truck, and taken to a market or grocery store. Most of the fruit is sent to factories, however.

Storing the fruit

Fruit keeps ripening after it is harvested. Some fruits can be stored and sold later. These fruits are kept in a dark, cool place to stop them from getting too ripe and rotting.

At the factory

Some fruit must be washed before it is sent to factories. Cherries cannot be washed until they arrive at the factories or they will rot.

These cherries are being sprayed with water on a conveyor belt. Washing the cherries removes any dirt, insects, or pesticides.

Workers at the factory sort through the washed fruit. They look for cherries that are rotten or damaged and throw them out.

The cherries are put into large buckets and frozen. They are then taken to other factories, where they will be packaged or used to make jam, juice, or pies.

Pesticides or helpful insects?

Pesticides kill insects and other pests that damage fruit trees, but they can also hurt the environment. Many farmers are trying to use pesticides less often to protect the environment and people's health. They are finding other, more natural ways to control pests and diseases.

Helpful creatures

Many fruit growers are bringing helpful insects, such as the ladybird beetle, into their orchards. These helpful insects eat many of the harmful ones, so the fruit grower can use less pesticide. This type of pest control is called **biological control**.

Too much pesticide?

Sometimes a fruit grower uses too much pesticide and accidentally kills helpful animals and insects. If too many helpful animals and insects are killed, the farmer must use even more pesticide.

Sometimes a fruit grower sprays too much pesticide to kill pests.

Helpful insects and animals eat the pests that have pesticide on them.

The pesticide kills the helpful creatures. They can no longer eat the pests.

The fruit grower must spray even more pesticide to kill pests.

Fruit is good for you!

Fruit is naturally sweet and delicious. It is also very **nutritious**, or good for you. Fruit contains vitamins that people need to make their body healthy and strong.

People use fruit in many different ways. We eat it fresh, from cans, and after it has been frozen. Fruit can be baked in desserts such as cherry pies or apple crisp. You can use fresh fruit at home to make many tasty and nutritious recipes.

Apple crisp

Here is a recipe that you can make at home. Ask an adult to help you when you use a knife or any kind of machine.

¾ cup (180 ml) brown sugar, packed

½ cup (125 ml) all-purpose flour

½ cup (125 ml) oats

¾ tsp (4 ml) each of cinnamon and nutmeg

⅓ cup (85 ml) margarine, softened

4 medium apples, cored, peeled, and sliced

Heat oven to 375° F (190° C). Grease a square pan and arrange the apple slices in it. In a bowl, mix the remaining ingredients thoroughly. Sprinkle over the apples. Bake for 30 minutes or until the apples are tender and the topping is golden brown.

Orchard words

bruise To dent the skin and flesh of fruit

drainage The removal of extra water from an orchard or a field

field A piece of land with few trees, on which fruits or vegetables are grown

grove A small group of trees without undergrowth

harvest To pick or gather up a crop

nutrient A nourishing substance found in food or soil

nutritious Describing food that contains things necessary for us to live and grow

pesticide A chemical used to destroy harmful plants or insects

pollinate To carry pollen from one flower to another so that seeds can be made

prune To remove branches from a tree to improve its shape and growth

ripe Describing a fruit that is fully grown and ready to be eaten

thin To pick fruit that is not fully grown so that there is more room for the remaining fruit to grow

vine A plant with a long stem that grows along the ground, on trees, or on walls

Index

1 2 3 4 5 6 7 8 9 0   Printed in the U.S.A. 6 5 4 3 2 1 0 9 8 7